AF281123

Mona von Maltzahn

Rêve bleu – The blue dream
Cultural highlights of the Côte d'Azur

With illustrations and photos by the author

Rêve bleu – The blue dream

Cultural highlights of the Côte d'Azur

Rêve bleu – The blue dream

Mona von Maltzahn

Cover photo: Cap Martin
Bibliographic information of the German National Library:
The German National Library lists this publication in the German National Bibliography; detailed bibliographic data is available on the Internet at http://dnb.dnb.de.

Translated from the German original edition published 2024 under
the title: Rêve bleu – Der blaue Traum
Many Thanks to K. Arthen

Publisher: BoD • Books on Demand GmbH, In de Tarpen 42,
22848 Norderstedt
Print: Libri Plureos GmbH, Friedensallee 273, 22763 Hamburg
ISBN: 978-3-7597-7906-9

Cultural highlights of the Côte d'Azur

For all lovers of the Côte d'Azur

Rêve bleu – The blue dream

Cultural highlights of the Côte d'Azur

Cultural highlights from Menton to Saint-Tropez

If you love the sea and appreciate art and culture, you will enjoy my cultural journeys to the French Riviera, experienced over decades. From Cocteau in Menton to Picasso in Antibes and Signac in Saint-Tropez, the carefully selected museums and cultural highlights offer inspiration and insights along the coast of southern France. Since the 18th century, the French Riviera has been a popular vacation destination for the French and tourists from all around the world.

The French Riviera is also known as Côte d'Azur. The name Côte d'Azur was coined by the poet Stéphen Liégeard, who published a book titled "La Côte d'Azur" in 1887. Côte means the cost and Azur is named after the azure, blue waters of this Riviera.

This book is an invitation to discover the incomparable beauty and diversity of the Côte d'Azur, where the azure, blue sea meets radiant culture. Every visit to the French Riviera promises unforgettable moments, enriching your senses with art, culture and the blue dream.

Cultural highlights of the Côte d'Azur

Menton

The first town after the Italian border is Menton. The city is famous for its lemons, parks, gardens, and picturesque, colorful houses. Here you'll find the Cocteau Museum - a modern building right on the beach next to the town hall.

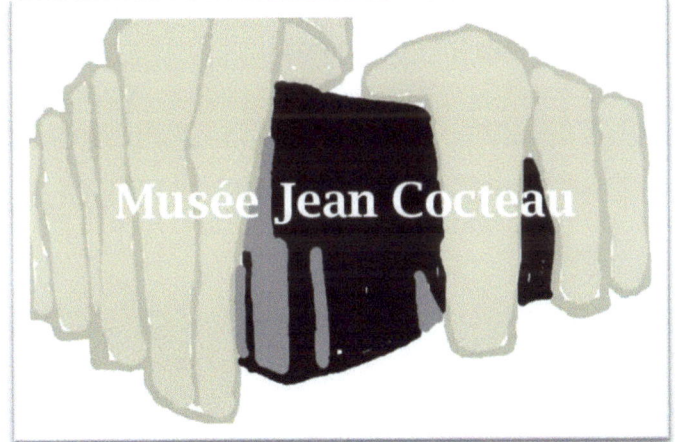

Illustration: Cocteau Museum

The Cocteau Museum (Musée Jean Cocteau) is dedicated to the French surrealist Jean Cocteau (1889-1963), a multitalented artist. He was a significant writer, painter, and filmmaker. The museum was built in 2011 according to the designs of French architect Rudy Ricciotti, a proponent of "hedonistic architecture." The result is impressive. Pierre Bergé, partner of the late Yves Saint Laurent, supported the construction of the museum.

In the nearby Bastion, a small fortress from 1619 overlooking the Mediterranean, is the original Cocteau Museum, which Cocteau helped design. Here you can view more works by the artist. The Cocteau Hall in Menton's town hall remains a popular wedding venue. Jean Cocteau left an indelible mark on Menton, shaping the city to this day. His works and influence are omnipresent, contributing to the cultural identity of this charming town. As you immerse yourself in Cocteau's world, you can also enjoy the culinary diversity and delicacies around the world-famous Menton lemons.

View of Cap Martin from Monaco

Between Menton and Monaco lies Roquebrune-Cap-Martin, with the Cap Moderne Museum and the house E-1027. For the museum tour, which involves steep and narrow coastal paths, good footwear is recommended. The small but spectacular hike to the museum offers fantastic views of the sea and Monaco.

Illustration: E-1027

The Cap Moderne Museum (Cap Moderne, Eileen Gray et Le Corbusier au Cap Martin) with the house E-1027 by Eileen Gray is a must for design lovers. E-1027 was designed and built in 1929 by Irish furniture designer Eileen Gray (1878-1976). It is a masterpiece of modern architecture and the Bauhaus movement.

The name E-1027 is a code containing the initials of Eileen Gray and her partner, the architect Jean Badovici: "E" for Eileen, "10" for Jean (the tenth letter of the alphabet), "2" for Badovici, and "7" for Gray. The famous modernist architect Le Corbusier (1887-1965), who was-friends with the designer couple, further developed the area and left significant traces of modern design.

The entire area around E-1027 was later declared a "Site Moderne," an area of cultural and historical significance and international interest.

View of Cap Martin from Roquebrune

Cultural highlights of the Côte d'Azur

Design maisonette in Roquebrune

Once, I stayed on the Cap Martin peninsula. The apartment was extraordinarily modern and located right on the steep main road with an exterior staircase that was spectacularly steep. Inside, the apartment was stylish, with round windows, a glass mezzanine, and elegant design elements—all in the style of Le Corbusier.

With clear lines and strict forms flooded with light, I could transport myself back to the time of the two designers in a frenzy of design.

Cultural highlights of the Côte d'Azur

Monaco

Monaco is only 5 km away, and there is no visible border between France and Monaco. The abundance of high-rise buildings, yachts, and luxury hotels is remarkable. Monaco is the second smallest state in the world. With an area of 0,8 square miles, it has about 40,000 residents, making it the most densely populated state in the world.

Place du Casino Monte-Carlo

As a student in the early 90s, hotels in Monaco were far beyond my financial reach. However, my friends and I still wanted to explore the city. Lacking money but full of curiosity and eagerness to learn, we slept in our old car on a side street in downtown Monte Carlo, which is no longer permitted. This allowed us to witness fantastic sunrises and be the first tourists in the city center. My highlights in Monaco are:

The Francis Bacon MB Art Foundation, located in the Villa Élise, is a foundation dedicated to the activities and research related to the art, life, and creative process of Francis Bacon. It has 3,500 objects, including the largest collection of early paintings and furniture by the artist. Francis Bacon (1909-1992) is considered one of the most significant figurative painters of the 20th century.

NMNM - Nouveau Musée National de Monaco has two locations:

The Villa Sauber and the Villa Paloma. Villa Sauber is one of the last Belle Époque villas in Monaco, while Villa Paloma was built in the early 20th century.

The collection includes works by Lucio Fontana, Andy Warhol, and Thomas Ruff. Both villas offer an impressive ambiance and regularly host changing exhibitions showcasing contemporary and modern art. Visitors can admire not only the artworks but also the architectural beauty and historical significance of the buildings.

The Oceanographic Museum of Monaco (Musée Océanographique de Monaco) is located on a cliff extending into the Mediterranean in the old town of Monaco. The museum exhibits thousands of marine creatures and offers interactive exhibition areas and educational programs, providing visitors of all ages with a fascinating and educational experience.

With its huge 6500 square meters of exhibition space, it feels for me like a temple of the sea.

Illustration: Oceanographic Museum of Monaco

View from the Oceanographic Museum

Cultural highlights of the Côte d'Azur

Cultural highlights of the Côte d'Azur

Èze

Èze is a picturesque village known for its medieval cobblestone streets and breathtaking views of the Mediterranean, attracting visitors from all over the world. The village offers a rich history, charming

Èze Village

boutiques, artisan shops, and traditional Provençal restaurants.

Often, my brother, his family, and I would hike up through the medieval village to the Botanical Garden.

There is no other place, which offers such a far-reaching and spectacular view of the sea as the open-air museum in Èze, Jardin Exotique d'Èze where the botanical garden is located.

During the Belle Époque, the first tourists in this area made the arduous climb from the sea to the castle ruins to enjoy the extraordinary vantage point.

After World War II, Jean Gastaud, the creator of the Exotic Garden in Monaco, established a fantastic exotic garden in Èze. The area is well-protected from northern winds by the Revère Plateau, making it a perfect spot for planting succulents such as cacti, agaves, and aloes.

View of the port of Monaco from Jardin du Casino

Situated over 400 meters above sea level, you can get a panoramic view from Cap Ferrat across the Esterel Massif to the Gulf of Saint-Tropez. The sky and sea meet, bathing everything in turquoise blue.

The statues by artist Jean-Philippe Richard turn the garden into an open-air museum. His earth maidens, named Chloé, Justine, Charlotte, Anaïs, Rose des vents, and Barbara, float between heaven and earth.

Illustration The botanic Garden Jardin Exotique d'Èze

Cultural highlights of the Côte d'Azur

Beaulieu sur Mer

Directly after Èze lies the beautiful town of Beaulieu-sur-Mer. I highly recommend to every art and culture enthusiast to plan a visit to Beaulieu. The town is picturesque, and from its beach, you can see two highlights of cultural history: Villa Kérylos and Villa Rothschild.

Illustration: Villa Kérylos

Villa Kérylos, designed in 1908 after ancient models by French architect and archaeologist Théodore Reinach, is now a museum. The villa is located directly by the sea at the tip of the bay of Beaulieu and boasts a beautiful garden. Entering it, you are enchanted by the view of the sea, the boats, the plants, the trees, the scent of jasmine, and the fantastic Greek-style villa.

Reinach created a unique monument to ancient Greece here, incorporating all the technical refinements available at the time. In 1966, Villa Kérylos was listed as a Monument historique and placed under heritage protection.

Illustration: Villa Rothschild

Villa Rothschild (Villa et Jardins Ephrussi de Rothschild) was completed in 1912 after five years of construction, commissioned by Baroness Béatrice de Rothschild on the Cap Ferrat peninsula. The building was constructed in the so-called Goût Rothschild ("Rothschild Taste"), a style popular in 19th-century France.

The museum housed within provides a vivid impression that the owners were great lovers of Belle Époque art. The collection is impressive, including several works from the Middle Ages and the Renaissance.

I particularly love the many meticulously maintained themed gardens, such as the Spanish and Japanese garden, the garden with many succulents, or the rose garden.

The baroness Rothschild bequeathed the villa to the Académie des Beaux-Arts, which opened it to the public in 1937.

On the way to Nice

Cultural highlights of the Côte d'Azur

Nice

Nice, one of the largest cities in France, was once home to the famous artist Henri Matisse. His house and studio are located here. The Matisse Museum (Musée Matisse) is situated on a hill in a quiet area of Nice, which is a pleasant retreat in this bustling city. Henri Matisse (1869-1954) is considered, along with Pablo Picasso, one of the most important artists of Classical Modernism.

Illustration: Matisse Museum

He is known as a pioneer and leading figure of Fauvism, turning away from Impressionism and representing the first artistic movement of the 20th century.

The museum's permanent collection includes many works that Matisse created from 1917 until his death in 1954 in Nice and left to the museum. The collection comprises paintings, drawings, prints, sculptures, illustrated books, and his famous paper cutouts.

Not far from the Matisse Museum is the Chagall Museum (Musée national Marc Chagall) which was founded during Marc Chagall's (1887-1985) lifetime and inaugurated in 1973.

It is also known as the "Musée National Message Biblique Marc Chagall" because it houses a series of seventeen paintings that illustrate the biblical message, painted by Chagall and donated to the French state in 1966.

Illustration: Chagall Museum

Marc Chagall personally provided detailed instructions for the garden's design and determined the placement of each of his works in the museum.

For those who wish to see originals by numerous significant artists in art history, the MAMAC in Nice is a must-visit. The museum features works by Yves Klein, the master of the color blue.

MAMAC Museum of Modern and Contemporary Art (Musée d'Art Moderne et d'Art Contemporain) is a museum of modern art that opened in 1990. The collection includes about 400 works from the 1960s onwards, featuring renowned artists such as Yves Klein, Niki de Saint-Phalle, Andy Warhol, and Tom Wesselmann.

Nice is home to two magnificent villas that showcase significant epochs in art history: the Belle Époque at Villa Masséna and the Baroque at Palais Lascaris.

Musée Villa Masséna is located on the Promenade des Anglais, one of the most famous promenades in the world, right next to the Hotel Negresco. Since 1921, it has presented art from the Belle Époque era as well as the art and regional history of the Côte d'Azur. The villa was built in 1902 according to the plans of Danish architect Hans-Georg Tersling. The building complex includes a large park designed in the English style but with Mediterranean plants.

Musée du Palais Lascaris is an aristocratic villa from the 17th century. Today, it is a museum of musical instruments, housing a collection of over 500 instruments, making it the second most important collection in France after the Musée de la Musique de la Philharmonie in Paris.

A visit to the flower and vegetable market in Nice is a feast for all senses, where the vibrant colors and fragrances of Provence beautifully come together.

Marché Aux Fleurs

Cultural highlights of the Côte d'Azur

Cagnes sur Mer

In Cagnes-sur-Mer, I once rented an apartment that was ideal for visiting Renoir's house. The Renoir Museum (Musée Renoir) is in a very

Lemon and orange trees in the garden of the Renoir Museum

idyllic villa with a beautiful park filled with impressive orange and lemon trees, offering a view of the sea. This is where the painter lived and worked.

Auguste Renoir (1841-1919) was one of the most important French painters of Impressionism. In his villa, he welcomed contemporaries such as Henri Matisse, Aristide Maillol, Amedeo Modigliani, Auguste Rodin, Pablo Picasso, and Claude Monet. Pierre-Auguste Renoir passed away at the age of 78, leaving behind around 6,000 works: landscapes, still lifes, portraits, nudes, as well as scenes of dance and family life.

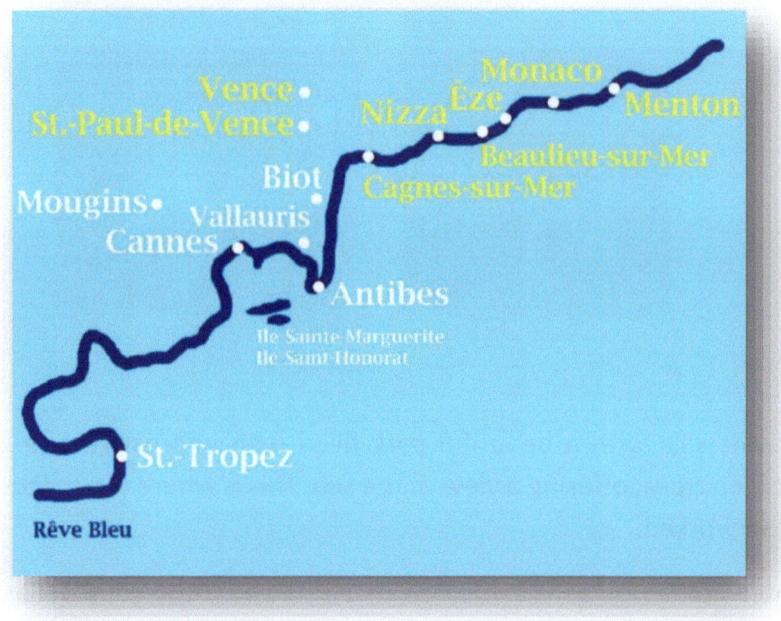

Cultural highlights of the Côte d'Azur

Vence / Saint-Paul-de-Vence

The "Rêve bleu" museum route now leads to the picturesque villages of Vence and Saint-Paul-de-Vence - two charming mountain villages straight out of a storybook.

Vence is famous for the Rosary Chapel of Vence (Chapelle du Rosaire de Vence), a masterpiece by Henri Matisse dating back to 1951.

The chapel is known for its blue and white roof, stained glass windows, and interior paintings featuring Matisse's Tree of Life.

In Saint-Paul-de-Vence, you'll find a haven for art lovers and the region's most beautiful museum, the Fondation Maeght. This foundation is an exhibition space for modern and contemporary art with a

33

sculpture garden. Founded by the Maeght couple, who were friends with artists like Miró, Picasso, Giacometti, Braque, Calder, Léger, and Chagall. In 1964, they set up a foundation to exhibit part of their collection there.

In collaboration with artists such as Joan Miró and Georges Braque, an ensemble of buildings was created that blends beautifully into the Mediterranean landscape.

The foundation owns an impressive number of masterpieces, including sculptures by Alberto Giacometti, works by Joan Miró as well as works by Alexander Calder, Fernand Léger, Marc Chagall, Wassily Kandinsky, Antoni Tàpies and many more. The integrated library is open to the public every day. It offers more than 30,000 volumes on modern and contemporary art.

The collection, which contains over 10,000 works, as well as the thematic exhibitions or retrospectives organized by the Fondation, attract visitors from all over the world every year.

A stay in Saint-Paul-de-Vence promises unforgettable experiences. Start your day with a stroll to the village and breakfast at Café de la Place, accompanied by the scent of jasmine and the gentle breeze. The unique light of the Côte d'Azur, which has inspired many artists, unfolds here in exquisite beauty.

Artist Village Saint-Paul-de-Vence

Cultural highlights of the Côte d'Azur

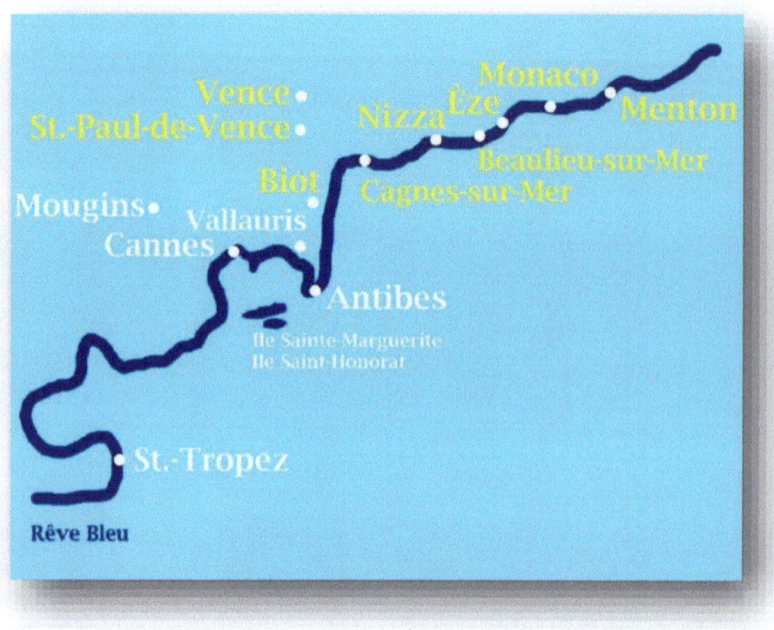

Cultural highlights of the Côte d'Azur

Biot

On the way from Saint-Paul-de-Vence to Antibes lies the picturesque village of Biot, just 4 km from the coast. In a big park there you can see the Léger Museum (Musée national Fernand-Léger).

Illustration: Fernand Léger

Fernand Léger (1881-1955) was a significant abstract artist. The museum in Biot houses the world's largest collection of his works, including paintings, drawings, ceramics, sculptures, stained glass windows, and tapestries. These artworks span all phases of his career from Impressionism through Cubism to precursors of Pop Art.

Notably, the museum's walls feature monumental mosaics that vividly depict Léger's works. Besides numerous paintings, Léger was also involved in decorating the United Nations headquarters in New York, underscoring his international significance.

Cultural highlights of the Côte d'Azur

Antibes

Antibes is one of the oldest cities on the Côte d'Azur, founded around 340 BC by the Greeks. The Picasso Museum (Musée Picasso Antibes) in Antibes is housed in a castle in the old town, right by the sea.

Illustration: Picasso Museum Antibes

In 1946, Picasso had his studio here and gifted the town with 23 paintings that are now displayed in the museum. He was later made an honorary citizen of Antibes.

39

Illustration: Picasso

Every time I see Picasso's portrait at the Picasso Museum in Antibes, I feel a sublime sensation. I imagine he is still alive, ready to come around the corner and recount tales from wartime and beyond, about how he seduced women and created his art. His childlike mischief and the lightness he exude have a mystical quality that resonates with this coast.

For me, amateur painting has always been a wonderful outlet for processing impressions and experiences. Most of my paintings have been inspired by the Coast of Light and the blue hues of the Côte d'Azur. Picasso has been my inspiration throughout.

In Antibes, you'll also find the Fondation Hartung-Bergmann, situated in a beautiful villa surrounded by olive trees. Hans Hartung (1904-1998), a significant German French painter and graphic artist of the 20th century, lived here with his wife, the Norwegian painter and graphic artist Anna-Eva Bergmann (1909-1987). The foundation documents the artistic legacy of this couple.

Antibes

Cultural highlights of the Côte d'Azur

Cultural highlights of the Côte d'Azur

Vallauris

Illustration: Picasso

Not far from Antibes lies the artist village of Vallauris. Known since the 16th century for its ceramics, Vallauris regularly hosts the International Biennial of Contemporary Ceramic Art.

In 1948, Pablo Picasso arrived here and created his masterpiece "War and Peace".

This work can be admired at the Museum Musée national Pablo Picasso La Guerre et la Paix.

Picasso also placed his bronze statue "Man with Sheep" from 1950 on the Vallauris marketplace.

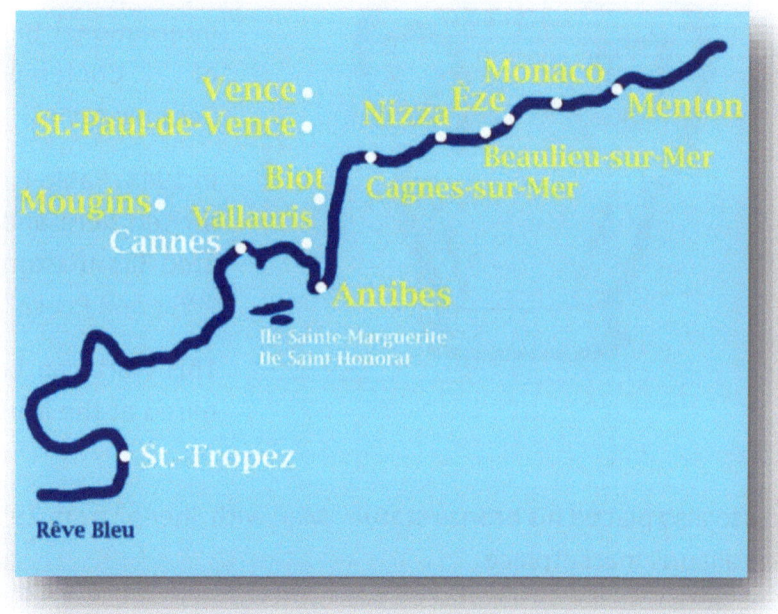

Cultural highlights of the Côte d'Azur

Mougins

Here in Mougins, one can still trace the footsteps of Picasso, where the great artist spent his final years before his death. This beautiful artist village feels like a painting itself. The expansive view of the untouched, wooded nature reserve with Europe's largest lotus colony and over 70 bird species is always a delight.

In the heart of the old village of Mougins lies the Centre de la photographie de Mougins. The former large rectory has been converted into a modern exhibition building, opened in 2021.

The museum includes a collection of photographs by André Villiers (1930-2016), who created many portraits of Picasso and his artist friends.

Illustration: Mougins

Cultural highlights of the Côte d'Azur

Cannes

Cannes, I always say, is the most glamorous trade fair and congress city in the world. It is bustling and boasts the most beautiful shopping street on the Côte d'Azur. Cannes, from Latin "canna" meaning reed, has always been a center of contemporary history.

.

Bay of Cannes

Cultural highlights of the Côte d'Azur

- Some key points about Cannes:
- 1815: Napoleon Bonaparte stays in Cannes on his return from Elba.
- 1834: Former British Lord Chancellor Henry Brougham discovers Cannes as a health resort.
- 1838: Construction of the Old Port.
- 1868: Construction of the Croisette, the famous promenade.
- 1912: Construction of the grand luxury hotels along the Croisette.
- 1946: The first Cannes International Film Festival takes place.

Beach restaurant on the Croisette in Cannes

Carousel on the Croisette

When I was 20 years old, I visited Cannes for the first time with a friend and his old Mercedes, eager cineastes on a mission to attend the film festival in May.

Cannes is a place for dreaming. I too spun my own dreams there. I dreamt of savoir-vivre, of buying flowers at the market with a wicker basket in hand, just like Jane Birkin. I dreamt of elegant scarves à la Grace Kelly and of a life filled with French music, where chansons sound beautifully melancholic and seem never-ending.

There are many memories and photos of Cannes. The city has remained true to itself over the years: very glamorous.

In the district Le Cannet,,on a hill is the Bonnard Museum (Musée Bonnard). Like Giverny for Claude Monet and Nice for Henri Matisse, Le Cannet was an important place for Pierre Bonnard.

Bonnard (1867-1947) purchased Villa Le Bosquet in 1926 and spent more than twenty years there. During this time, he painted his inspiring works that experts consider his finest pieces.

Illustration: Bonnard

Bonnard, who developed his own style of painting from the Post Im-pressionist art movement, created an important cultural institution on the Côte d'Azur with the Bonnard Museum.

In Cannes, there's much to discover. La Malmaison Museum in the city center, surrounded by grand hotels, is noteworthy for its modern art exhibitions.

Cultural highlights of the Côte d'Azur

Île de Sainte-Marguerite / Île de Saint-Honorat

The two islands off Cannes are Île de Saint Marguerite and Île de Saint Honorat:

Île de Sainte-Marguerite with its impressive Fort Royal, a state prison for several centuries, is worth a visit. The most famous prisoner there in 1698 was the mysterious "Man in the Iron Mask", whose identity remains partially unresolved.

View of the Islands from Cannes

Île de Saint-Honorat houses the beautiful Monastery Abbey of Lérins with its well-preserved fortified tower.

The monks who reside there produce their own wine.

The restaurant on the island comes highly recommended. You can reach the islands by ferry from Cannes in just 15 minutes and enjoy the view of the mainland.

The influences of numerous tourists over the centuries, the exile of artists and writers, and the many people who came to the Côte d'Azur

seeking inspiration continue to shape the region to this day.

You can feel it in every alley, on the streets, and in the faces of the residents, in their pride and love for beauty.

For me, all of this embodies the true essence of the French Riviera.

Estérel mountains

Théoule-sur-Mer is a small town after Cannes where I spent many summers studying art routes. The town is famous for the Pierre Cardin house Palais Bulles.

The coast from Cannes towards Saint-Tropez now takes on a reddish hue. The Estérel Mountains with their red rocks form a beautiful backdrop against the deep blue sea.

On the way from Théoule-sur-Mer to Saint-Tropez

Passing many places with evocative names like Fréjus, Saint-Raphaël, or Sainte-Maxime, you reach Saint-Tropez. Many years later, I lived in the Bay of Saint-Tropez in an old house in the small village of Les Issambres, which I named Rêve bleu (The Blue Dream).

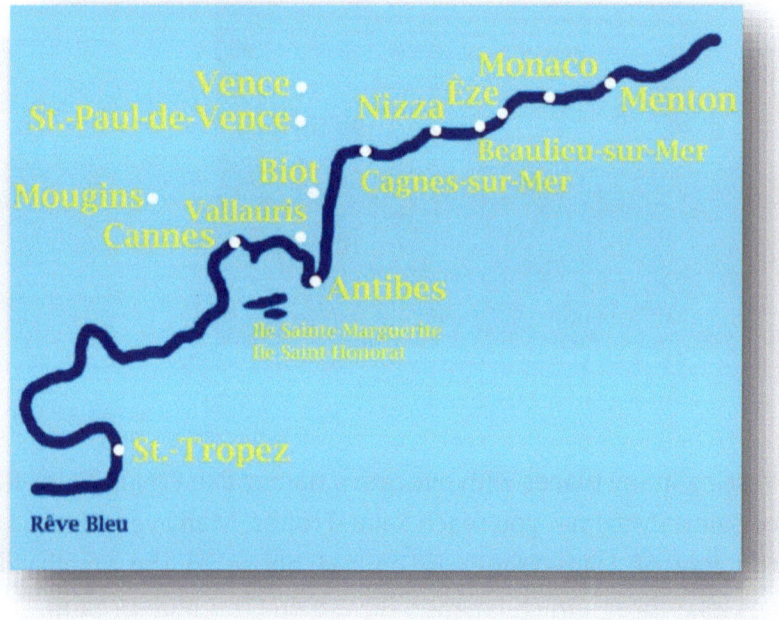

Cultural highlights of the Côte d'Azur

Saint-Tropez

Saint-Tropez, named after Saint Torpes, a martyr, was until the 20th century a simple fishing village.

Today, it is a magnet for people from around the world.

Illustration: Signac

The Musée de l'Annonciade, an art museum right on the port of Saint-Tropez, mainly exhibits artworks from the 19th and 20th centuries. The art collection is housed in a former 16th-century chapel.

A focus here is on works by artists who worked in Saint-Tropez or found their inspiration in the Mediterranean landscape.

Paul Signac (1863-1935) lived and worked in Saint-Tropez. Initially in-spired by Claude Monet and the Impressionists, he later developed Pointillism, a new style. Signac was the first artist to come to Saint-Tropez in 1892, followed by many others who appreciated the charm of the place and captured it in their works.

Pablo Picasso painted "L'Odalisque" here. Bernard Buffet, Massimo Campigli, David Hockney, and many others also lived and worked in Saint-Tropez.

Very beautiful here is the landmark of Saint-Tropez La Citadelle. The fortress above the city is a hexagonal, imposing structure from the 16th century. Here you'll find the Maritime History Museum La Citadelle de Saint-Tropez – Musée d'histoire maritime, which also docu-ments the history of Saint-Tropez.

Saint-Tropez

Cultural highlights of the Côte d'Azur

The beaches in the hinterland of Saint-Tropez on the peninsula are surrounded by numerous myths and stories.

They have served as picturesque settings for several movies. Generations of artists, celebrities and bohemians with a unique lifestyle have found inspirations and ideas for their big dreams.

Here is the end of my cultural journey "Rêve Bleu", which can also serve as the beginning of a new blue dream on the French Riviera.

ADDRESSES OF THE CULTURAL HIGHLIGHTS:

Rêve bleu – The blue dream

Cultural highlights of the Côte d'Azur

Menton

Musée Jean Cocteau

www.museecocteaumenton.fr

Quai Napoléon III – Bastion du Vieux Port
06500 Menton

Cap Moderne, Eileen Gray et Le Corbusier au Cap Martin

www.capmoderne.monuments-nationaux.fr

Esplanade de la Gare SNCF de Cap-Martin
Roquebrune
Avenue Le Corbusier
06190 Roquebrune Cap Martin

Monaco

Francis Bacon MB Art Foundation - Villa Élise

www.mbartfoundation.com

21 boulevard d´Italie, Monaco

NMNM - Nouveau Musée National de Monaco-
Villa Sauber

www.nmnm.mc

17 avenue Princesse Grace, Monaco

NMNM - Nouveau Musée National de Monaco -
Villa Paloma

www.nmnm.mc

56 boulevard du Jardin Exotique, Monaco

Musée Océanographique de Monaco

www.musee.oceano.org

avenue Saint-Martin, Monaco

Èze

Jardin Exotique d'Èze

www.jardinexotique-eze.fr

Rue du Château
06360 Eze

Beauliau sur Mer

Villa Kérylos

www.villakerylos.fr

Impasse Gustave Eiffel
06310 Beaulieu-sur-Mer

Villa et Jardins Ephrussi de Rothschild

www.villa-ephrussi.com

1 Av. Ephrussi de Rothschild
06230 Saint-Jean-Cap-Ferrat

Nice

Musée Matisse

www.musee-matisse-nice.org

164, avenue des Arènes de
Cimiez
06000 Nice

Musée national Marc Chagall

www.musees-nationaux-
alpesmaritimes.fr

Avenue du Docteur Ménard
06000 Nice

MAMAC – Musée d'Art Moderne et d'Art Contemporain

www.mamac-nice.org

Place Yves Klein
06300 Nice

Musée Villa Masséna

www.nice.fr

65, rue de France
06000 Nice

Musée du Palais Lascaris

www.nice.fr

15, rue Droite
06300 Nice

Cagnes sur Mer

Musée Renoir

www.tourisme.cagnes.fr

19, Chemin des Collettes
06800 Cagnes sur Mer

Vence / Saint-Paul-de-Vence

Chapelle du Rosaire de Vence

www.chapellematisse.com

466 Avenue Henri Matisse
06140 Vence

Fondation Maeght

www.fondation-maeght.com

623 Chemin des Gardettes
06570 Saint-Paul

Biot

Musée national Fernand-Léger

www.musees-nationaux-alpesmaritimes.fr

255, chemin du Val-de-Pôme
06410 Biot

Antibes

Musée PicassoAntibes

www.antibesjuanlespins.com

place mariejol
06600 Antibes

Fondation Hartung-Bergman

www.fondationhartungbergman.fr

173, chemin du Valbosquet

06600 Antibes

Vallauris

Musée national Pablo Picasso, La Guerre et La Paix

www.musees-nationaux-alpesmaritimes.fr

1, Place de la Libération du 24 Août 1944
06220 Vallauris

Mougins

Centre de la photographie de Mougins

www.centrephotographiemougins.com

43, rue de l'Église
06250 Mougins

Cannes

Musée Bonnard

www.museebonnard.fr

16, boulevard Sadi Carnot
06110 Le Cannet

La Malmaison

www.cannes.com/fr/culture/musees-et-
expositions/la-malmaison.html

47, boulevard de la Croisette
06400 Cannes

Île de Sainte-Marguerite / Île de Saint-Honorat

Royal Fort

https://exploretheriviera.com/ile-sainte-marguerite-
cannes-guide/

Abbaye de Lérins

www.abbayedelerins.com

Saint-Tropez

Musée de l'Annonciade

www.saint-tropez.fr

2, place Georges Grammont
83990 Saint Tropez

La Citadelle de Saint-Tropez – Musée d'histoire maritime

www.saint-tropez.fr

1, montée de la Citadelle
83990 Saint-Tropez

Cultural highlights of the Côte d'Azur

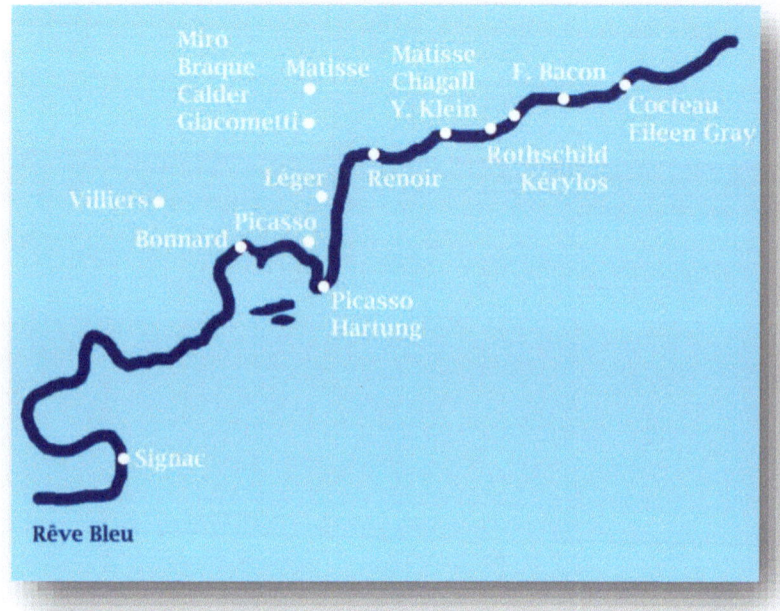

Cultural highlights of the Côte d'Azur

List of Artists: